SUPER SURPRISING TRIVIA ABOUT ANCIENT CIVILIZATIONS

by Lisa M. Bolt Simons

CAPSTONE PRESS
a capstone imprint

Spark is published by Capstone Press, an imprint of Capstone
1710 Roe Crest Drive, North Mankato, Minnesota 56003
capstonepub.com

Library of Congress Cataloging-in-Publication Data
Names: Simons, Lisa M. Bolt, 1969– author.
Title: Super surprising trivia about ancient civilizations / by Lisa M. Bolt Simons.
Description: North Mankato, Minnesota : Capstone Press, an imprint of Capstone, [2024] | Series: Super surprising trivia you can't resist | Includes bibliographical references and index. | Audience: Ages 9-11 | Audience: Grades 4-6 | Summary: "Think you know a lot about ancient civilizations? Prepare to learn even more about the people of the ancient world and the surprising details of their cities, people, and daily lives. You'll be surprised by how much you'll discover in this totally terrific book of trivia about ancient civilizations"— Provided by publisher.
Identifiers: LCCN 2023000345 (print) | LCCN 2023000346 (ebook) | ISBN 9781669050230 (hardcover) | ISBN 9781669071631 (paperback) | ISBN 9781669050193 (ebook pdf) | ISBN 9781669050216 (kindle edition) | ISBN 9781669050223 (epub) Subjects: LCSH: Civilization, Ancient—Miscellanea—Juvenile literature. | History, Ancient—Miscellanea—Juvenile literature. Classification: LCC CB311 .S56 2024 (print) | LCC CB311 (ebook) | DDC 930—dc23/eng/20230111
LC record available at https://lccn.loc.gov/2023000345
LC ebook record available at https://lccn.loc.gov/2023000346

TABLE OF CONTENTS

Super Ancient Civilizations 4

Mesopotamia 6

Ancient Egypt 12

Ancient India 16

Ancient Meso-America and South America 22

Ancient China 26

Glossary 30

Read More 31

Internet Sites. 31

Index 32

About the Author. 32

Words in **bold** are in the glossary.

SUPER ANCIENT CIVILIZATIONS

A civilization is made up of people living and working together in communities. These communities can be connected over a large area. **Ancient** civilizations began about 6,000 years ago.

How do we know about ancient civilizations? People have found **ruins** and even writings. Humans invented writing more than 5,000 years ago.

Ruins in present-day Turkey

MESOPOTAMIA

Mesopotamia is considered the oldest civilization in the world. People in the Sumer **region** of Mesopotamia invented writing.

People there didn't have paper. They had clay. These Sumerians used a **stylus** to press messages into clay.

Sumerians made the first calendar. It was based on phases of the moon. The first day of the month started on the first day the moon appeared.

Mesopotamia had one of the first legal systems. King Hammurabi of Babylon created 282 laws for people in Mesopotamia. It was called the Code of Hammurabi.

The Code of Hammurabi carved into a statue

Mesopotamia was the start of other things we use today. The wheel was first invented here. But it wasn't used for transportation. It was used to make pottery.

a potter's wheel

People here were also the first to make glass objects.

ANCIENT EGYPT

Pharaohs ruled Ancient Egypt. Most were male. But some, like Nefertiti, were female.

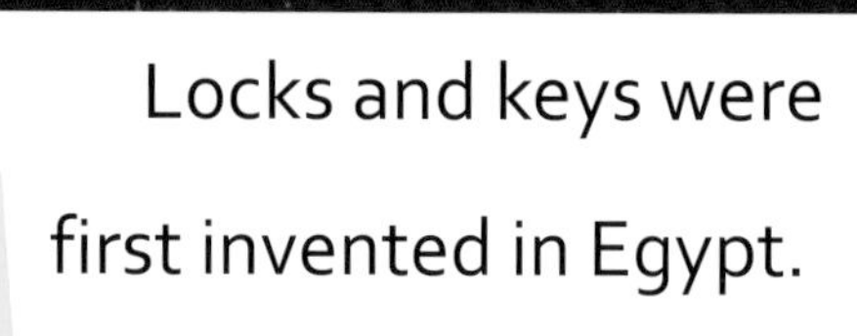

Locks and keys were first invented in Egypt.

Ancient Egyptians played board games. One looked a bit like checkers.

Some ancient Egyptian women wore wigs. Wigs were made of human hair or vegetable fiber.

In ancient Egypt, both women and men wore makeup.

Ancient Egypt had doctors. Most studied special areas, such as the brain or the heart. Some were even dentists.

ANCIENT INDIA

Ancient Indians were math masters. Have you ever celebrated **Pi** Day by eating pie? Thank them! They discovered the mathematical **concept** of pi.

Indians also first created the **decimal system**.

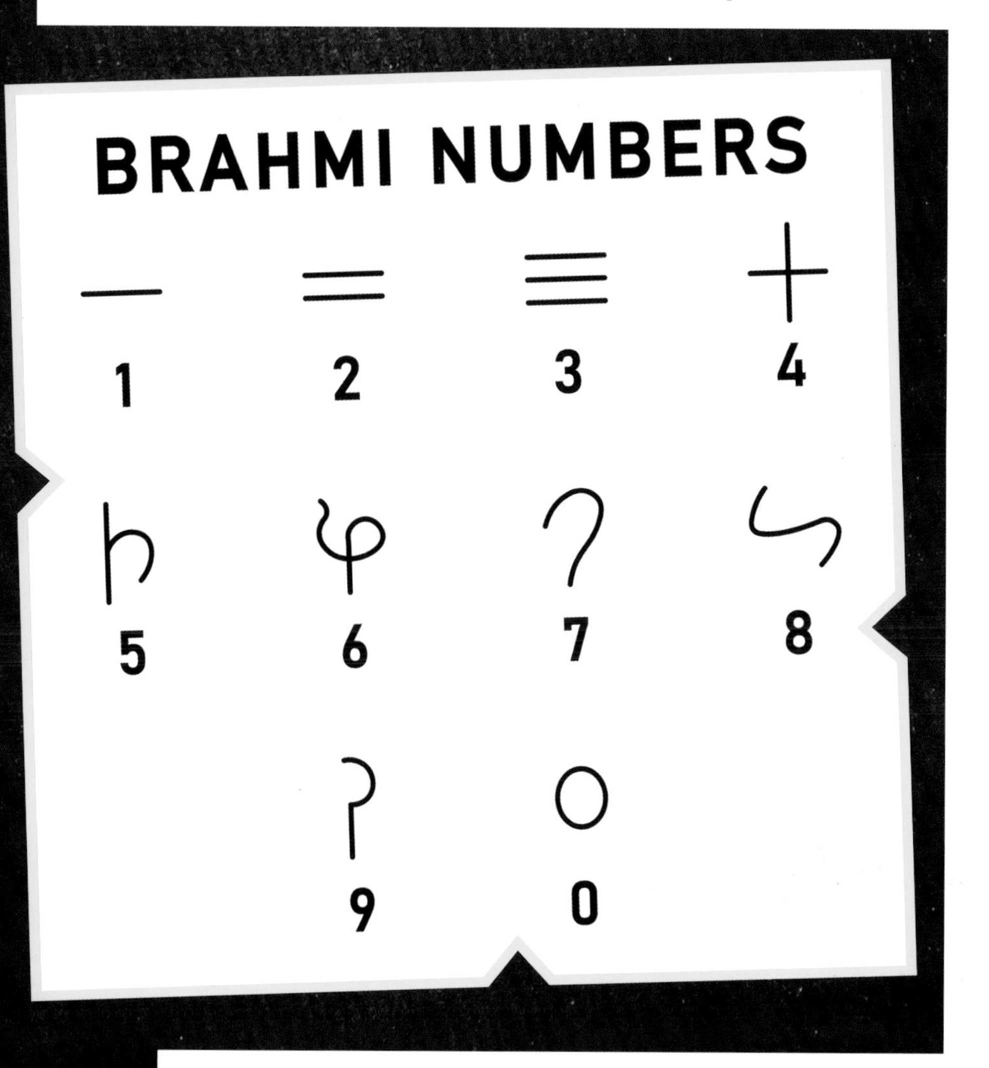

The idea of zero was invented in India 1,200 years ago.

Around 4,000 years ago, Indians were probably the first people to raise chickens.

How many of your clothes are made from cotton? Ancient Indians made their clothes from cotton too.

Have you ever tried yoga? This exercise comes from India. It's more than 5,000 years old!

Ancient Indians had toilets kind of like modern ones.

Shampoo was invented by ancient Indians.

ANCIENT MESO-AMERICA and SOUTH AMERICA

The Mayans and Incas lived in Central America 2,000 years ago. Both civilizations built beautiful **structures**. They made pyramids, palaces, and even **fortresses**.

Machu Picchu

The Incas developed a 14,000-mile road system. It connected their communities.

Mayan temples

The Inca Trail

Our writing system has 26 characters. The Mayans' had more than 800. They wrote on paper, stone, and pottery.

The Incas didn't have a writing system. They tied knots in colored strings to communicate.

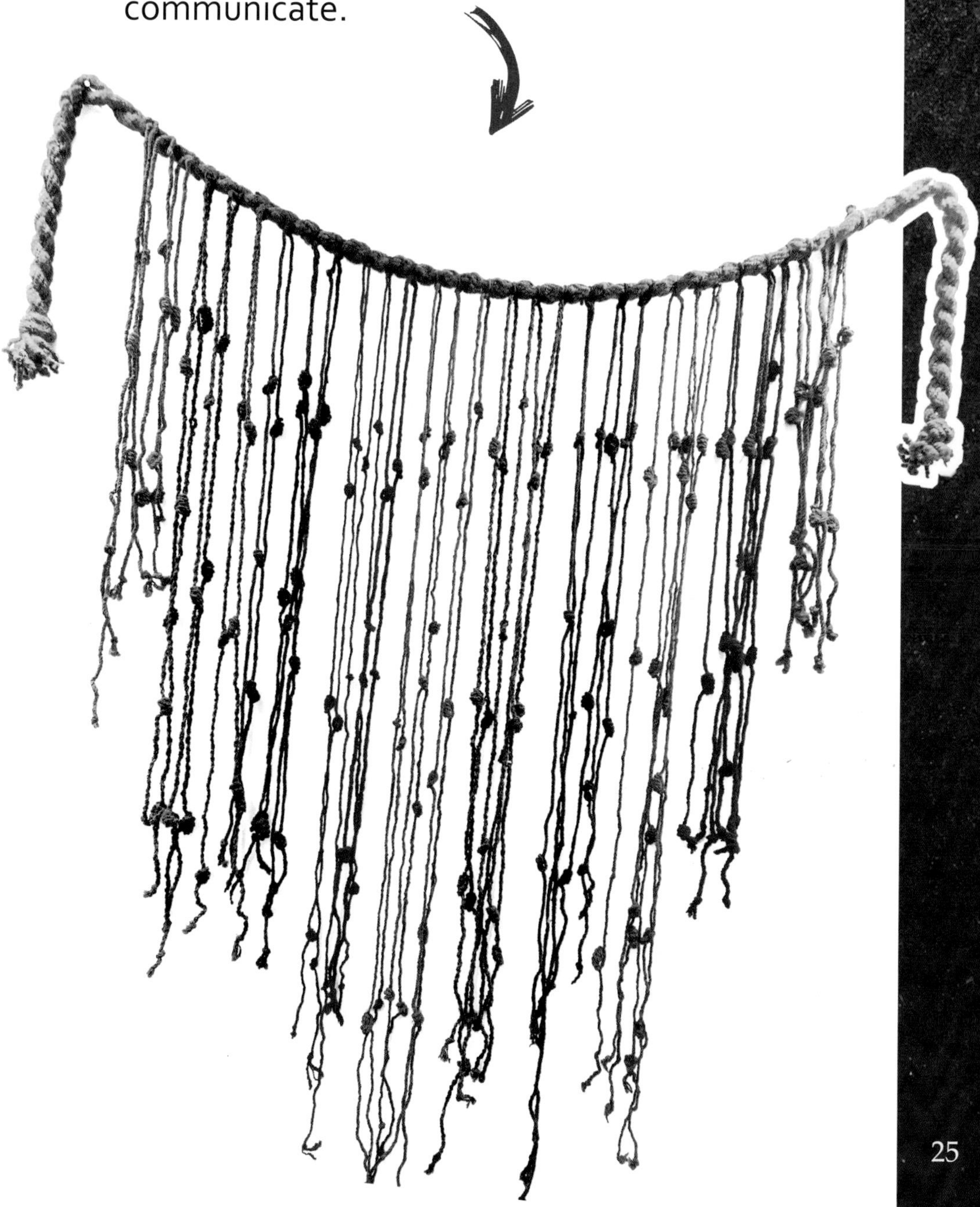

ANCIENT CHINA

About 5,000 years ago, the ancient Chinese had settled in the Yellow River valley. They mastered silk-making.

Starting about 700 years ago, the Great Wall of China was built. It protected China from outside armies. It would take more than a year to walk its full distance!

Paper was first made in China in the year 105. Papermakers used plant fibers, rags, and water.

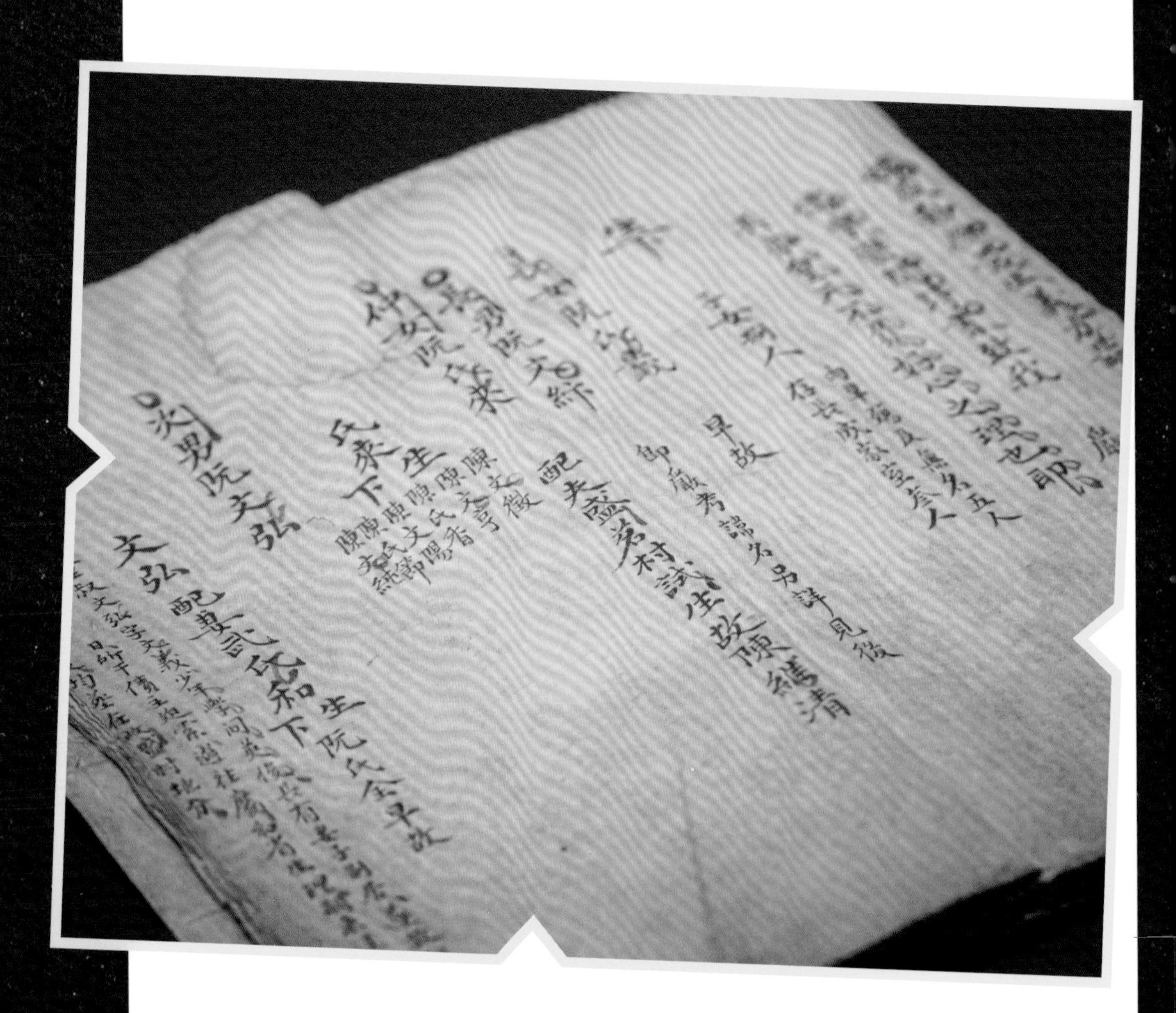

About 500 years later, China was the first country to use a printing press. What do you think kids in ancient China read about?

Glossary

ancient (AYN-shunt)—from a long time ago

concept (KAHN-sept)—an idea for a new way to build, create, or understand something

decimal system (DESS-uh-muhl SISS-tuhm)—a system of counting and computation that has the number 10 as its base

fortress (FOR-triss)—a place that is strengthened against attack

pi (PYE)—in math, a symbol for the ratio, or fraction, that represents the circumference of a circle compared to its diameter, or width; pi equals 3.1416

region (REE-juhn)—a large area

ruins (ROO-ins)—the remains of a building or other things that have fallen down or been destroyed

structure (STRUHK-chur)—something that has been built, such as a house, pyramid, or fortress

stylus (STY-luhs)—an ancient writing instrument made of bone, metal, or the like

Read More

Green, Sara. *Ancient Mesopotamia*. Minneapolis: Bellwether Media Inc., 2020.

McManus, Lori. *Ancient Civilizations: Women Who Made a Difference*. New York: Children's Press, an imprint of Scholastic Inc., 2022.

Nardo, Don. *Ancient Egypt*. New York: AV2, 2021.

Oachs, Emily Rose. *Ancient China*. Minneapolis: Bellwether Media Inc., 2020.

Internet Sites

Britannica Kids: Ancient Civilization.
kids.britannica.com/students/article/ancient-civilization/272856#196361-toc

National Geographic Kids: Seven Wonders of the Ancient World
kids.nationalgeographic.com/history/article/seven-wonders

The History of Paper
afandpa.org/news/2021/history-paper

Index

calendars, 8
Code of Hammurabi, 9
cotton, 19

doctors, 15

games, 13
glass objects, 11
Great Wall of China, the, 27

Incas, 22, 23, 25

locks and keys, 12

Machu Picchu, 22
makeup, 14
math, 16, 17
Mayans, 22, 23, 24

paper, 7, 24, 28
Pharaohs, 12
    Nefertiti, 12
pottery, 10, 24
printing press, 29

silk, 26
Sumerians, 6, 7, 8

toilets, 21

wigs, 14
writing, 4, 6, 7, 24, 25

yoga, 20

About the Author

@Jillian Raye Photography

Lisa M. Bolt Simons has published more than 60 nonfiction children's books and middle grade novels, as well as an adult history title. She's received accolades for both her nonfiction and fiction. Originally from Colorado, she currently resides in a town of 140 in Minnesota. She's a mom to adult girl/boy twins and is a wife to a book-loving guy.